SPLINTER

poems

Also by Susan O'Dell Underwood

Poetry

The Book of Awe (2018)

Poetry Chapbooks

From (2010)
Love and Other Hungers (2014)

Fiction

Genesis Road (2022)

SPLINTER

poems

Susan O'Dell Underwood

LAKE DALLAS, TEXAS

Requests for permission to reprint or reuse material from this work
should be sent to:

Permissions
Madville Publishing
PO Box 358
Lake Dallas, TX 75065

Cover Design and Photo: David Underwood
Author Photo: David Underwood

ISBN: 9781956440294 paperback and 9781956440300 ebook
Library of Congress Control Number: 2022944373

with gratitude to my people,
who gave me both roots and voice—

CONTENTS

IV. Gentrification

SPLINTER

poems

Appalachian Diaspora

Such wind this April afternoon might pluck
the blowsy-headed white oak
from the ridgeline, easy as a clover.

Or: watch the tree pull itself
up by the roots, lift helium-headstrong into blue
and skirt the ground untethered,
dragging roots and musk and moss.
The crown of tousled branches doesn't hesitate,
tugging the vertical ballast of the bole.
A lumbering whimsy pure as infancy.

Which part to blame, the rootwad
or those mulish heaving limbs?
Or the naive, prescient buds?

It's impossible to surge back into those sockets,
dark with their *I told you so.*

Name what prodigal welcome home
is ever worth the leaving
after the aerial view
of every lovely other across the blue
upon blue mountains?
Anyway, what a plunging crash it would take
to midwife those sweet, sap-drenched ropey lengths
back into the hollows healing over.

A wish invents itself and goes.
A sort of normal nothing comes from hanging on.
A sort of anguish crops up where the rich soil aches,
a beckoning *against* as much as *toward.*
The wandering gesture fills the air which gives in
like a cave, where forests used to bloom.

I. Holler

Holler

I saw the best minds of my generation outsourced, exported from the
Mountain South, lured by the shiny metropolis,
seduced by suburban retail and big salaries and common ground
with people who never heard of Appalachia,
or who pronounce it wrong.
My cousins hightailed it out of here—
the epidemiologist in San Francisco, curator of master drawings in
Rome, the librarian, corporate lawyer, NASA consultant, geneticist,
marine biologist, the naval officer in Hawaii,
my engineer brother designing war weaponry in Texas,
all of them flying home for holidays and funerals
of relatives who never once stepped foot on a plane.
They count me lucky, to keep on living here, where the standards
(they say to my face) are low, at least.
They say I'm an enviable two-hour drive from where our family
land—still in the family—runs from hill to hill, in a holler
cut through by the South Holston River.
They say they're jealous, of my meager house with English ivy and
moss, my brief walk on cracked sidewalks to my college office,
past defunct, rundown, boarded-up small town drear.
They say at least I'm geographically close to home.
Same as I do, they still call it *home* but don't realize
I'm not any closer to those roots than they are,
that I might as well be as far gone as any of them in exile,
that the leftover family land isn't deeded to me,
that the family that was ours is mostly dead and gone anyway,
that the culture they idealize is past, as distant from me as it is from them,
my head in a book instead of bumping a cow's udder;
my life behind a desk instead of behind a plow;
my yard full of shade trees and grass to mow,
no front porch, no back porch, no room or sun to grow a garden,
even if I knew how;
my house with internet cables connecting me to students
who ask in emails about the region's literature I've assigned:
What's an outhouse? What's fatback? What's a pig in a poke?

In dark days I ask myself why it has to be me left to teach
what's history now, why me,
keeping the antique stories and old names of this part of the country,
Appalachia, America, as if the language and terrain
were barbwired into me,
when some days, I swear, I'd just as soon put to some other use
in some other place the future my ancestors pictured for me,
hopeful I'd have a better, easier, more refined life than theirs, than this.
Even right here, I live in my time, though.
I need skills they'd never have dreamed, merging into interstate traffic,
booking hotel rooms that cost what an acre of land used to,
standing in line for a latte,
taking subways and metros and buses when I get out in the *real world*.
I have done as much as I could
to earn and enjoy my peoples' sacrifices before me.
I have obtained the highest degree in my field.
I have taken a train through the Alps and flown in a jet over Greenland,
and I have stood in the Colosseum in Rome
and seen the *Mona Lisa* in the Louvre.
I have hiked the Wonderland Trail at Mt. Rainier
and stood in the cold Pacific.
I have ordered sushi in Kansas City
while I listened to jazz I could understand fine,
           and I've eaten calamari right out of Monterey Bay
with just the right wine.
And I know which fork to use for my salad.
I have driven through the Holland Tunnel and gone to Broadway plays,
           and I've eaten a slice in Brooklyn and a knish in Central Park.
I have read—and taught—the finest books ever written
and learned when I was young to play the piano.
I know Beethoven from Mozart,
I know suri alpaca from cashmere, fine bourbon from fine Scotch,
polenta from spoon bread,
mac and cheese from pasta quattro formaggi.
I have seen and smelled and tasted as far as I can get from where I
was raised, so far I think I can't stand ever to go home again,
and so far I panic I'll never get all the way back home again.

There are some days when I know I'm lucky I can't ever escape,
that it's my duty, my call right here to teach kids
who are the first in their families to go to college.
They read sonnets and write essays about sonnets,
and soon they're tempted against their will to write sonnets,
and stories, and papers on Faulkner and Foucault.
All the time, running in place—this place—they are leaving
a little bit, never suspecting my ruse, my real agenda:
that someday their parents and cousins and grandparents will say
goodbye to them because I have helped prove
that they are smart and strong enough
to leave our beautiful, heartbreaking hills,
that they've been born and raised to get the hell out,
nothing for them here,
no cyber-commute far enough,
no library big enough to contain them,
no museum that's going to quench their desire for color, color, color,
no cocktail party too sophisticated,
not to mention noise and lights and big paychecks
        and every rich taste at their hungry fingertips.
Like them, I have been starved every day of my life,
thinking I should just sell my birthright, get out while I still can,
thinking sometimes I've been a rube, cheated, left behind in
podunkville, bohunk, poverty-ridden low-class, back end of beyond,
rural know-nothing nowhere.

And I have ordered expensive shoes online
to try and make up the difference.
And on the phone I change my accent with telemarketers and pollsters
        I have no reason to impress.
I have lowered my voice and ducked my head and grinned
and felt murderous when, in other places, I speak
and people look at me with surprise and disappointment
and ask me where I'm from,
as if the mother ship has landed,
as if I've arrived with a pone of cornbread in my hand
and lice in my hair and an ignorant, dullard brain in my head.

America, my students
who don't believe there's a class division, a pecking order,
a hard road ahead,
who disdain the housekeepers in their dorms,
who make fun of poor whites, trailer trash, rednecks,
who go on mission trips to *impoverished* places
like Haiti and India and rural China,
who don't recognize the sounds of their own prejudice
anymore than they recognize their own poor grammar,
look at me with confusion when I tell them:
You sweet naive children, dear darlings
for whom I've sacrificed a different kind of life,
        you are and always will be somebody's hillbilly.

America, Appalachia gave up nothing to you in its timber, its coal,
its dignity, nothing compared to giving you its children,
whom you will begrudgingly agree to take,
if they straighten up and dumb down their ways,
and even out their hick accents,
        and smarten up their acts, and blend and homogenize.
America, I'm not here like my ancestors
who made charcoal and pig iron that started this country.
I'm not here digging out coal or zinc, or lobbying for or against
strip mining or mountaintop coal removal,
although I know you are still up to your tricks.
I'm not picketing your coal-burning plants
that muddy up my air while you breathe clean,
or protesting the hydroelectric dams that broke our rivers.
I'm not logging forests—like my granddaddy who built your furniture.
I'm not raising any tobacco—like my daddy did—
to put me through school.
I'm not making quilts or weaving baskets—like my grandmothers
did—for you to buy on vacation.
I'm not preaching Jesus or hellfire.
I'm not handling any snakes or distilling moonshine
(which you like to read about).
I'm not playing a banjo or fiddle
or singing any godforsaken, melancholy ballad.
What I'm doing is way more dangerous, teaching a bunch of kids:

that the brains God gave them are for something
besides Vols football stats and NASCAR drivers' numbers;
that they grew up on the front lines,
set by the Deists and the Calvinists we sprang from right here,
where freedom of and from religion are still put to the test;
that faith and evolution coexist
with God the Father and Jesus the Son, Amen.
That we've been called backward and barbarian and heathen and
simple and quaint and lazy and uncivilized—
a hybrid, mongrel, monstrous underclass;
that they get to decide what to call themselves next;
that they have a choice.
But that to misplace their commas and semicolons might create
a bigger dividing line than they can imagine,
that to avoid sentence fragments and agreement errors
might save their lives,
that they should learn not to say, "I seen him go over the ridge," or
"when we've went to town," or
"my mama and them says to tell you hey,"
and that they should never dare
correct their grandparents or parents for saying the same.

I spend hours marking their every error I can catch,
using all the energy I have without giving away
how truly terrified I am for them,
of the possible dead-end hourly pay
and time-clock-punching that's historically, nearly unavoidably theirs,
of the threat of a vertical backyard
behind the double-wide trailer of their futures, or of a future
they might spend like me, a traitor,
teaching the next generation to leave.

America, I'm getting them as ready as I can
to climb onto that airplane or Greyhound,
or into their daddy's Hemi pickup, or to hitch a ride
with somebody eastbound, westbound, northbound,
to put on their boots and take up their beds and U-Haul it out of here.
America, I'm putting my hillbilly shoulder to the wheel.

II. Farmers' Daughter

Ghazal of the Farmers' Daughter

The start of all I knew was land where we were Everybody—
children, dogs, uncles, cousins, mules, aunts—a name for every body.

Between the river and the sinks-of-the-branch, hay wagons
like rafts across the fields at dusk carried home everybody.

Supper sang. And after, there was still more work to be done,
with buckets and bridles. Soft dark wavered with the satellites of bodies.

At the barn, my brother thought the calf at the cow's udder
nipped her fingers. He mistook the earnest yoke between two bodies.

The old ones tall above us laughed, and Papa showed him: *teats*,
bending down to shoulder into the mama cow's warm body.

The ones who fed us gathered eggs, kept gardens, stayed with green
and blood, the vital raising up and butchering of bodies.

I stood at the fencerow myself, to water Angus cattle at their trough.
As they drank distracted, I would touch the warm hide of their bodies.

Their noses slung snot. Manure-mucked asses twitched against flies.
I loved their black, pure eyes, their heavy, lumbering bodies.

But I never thought about which one we ate, roast salt and sirloin pink.
Not love but sacrifice back then went blind to the gifts of the body.

I took for granted those fields of grasses, marrow to marrow,
muscle and heart, bones that made my bones to carry this body.

Earthbound

Everybody lived closer to the ground then.
Not just kids and babies trundling free-range
& farm dogs in the shaded dirt
& chickens pecking.
Even aunts and uncles who worked in town
came home each night to milk cows & slop hogs & hoe
as many rows as they could before full dark.

Clods big as a man's fist, I could bust those up
in seconds with my two small hands—red clay,
brown loam—dried halfway to stone to dare me.
Every time I won & followed triumph
after triumph in the rows
until my feet & knees & palms went raw.

Were the ones I looked to
like me, charmed in that bending, leaning, kneeling,
raising up in sweaty praise?
Did they wish they could have chosen another way?

We all lie down to die some place or other.
Would they sometimes think of being
buried when they stumbled in the dredged-up furrows?
Or did they simply live to the end of every row?
Did they think of questions they might have asked
their dead, as I ask now?

The fields grown up in grass & clover
never speak.
There's nothing earth healed over
over them can ever answer me.

Tick

Cruelty went by other names:
necessity, caution, tradition.
My daddy would haul a hound dog to his side,
ribcage firm against ribcage,
and with his free hand search along the short-haired hide
to find each tick stuck like a backward
bloody nipple, suckling, full enough to burst.
The old dogs never skittish of the sulfur smell,
the match he struck burning close enough
to shrivel the tick's legs and then the tick.
And I was never skittish either,
nuzzling the young pups nose to nose,
calming them that it would be okay.
I couldn't help wanting to watch each tortured,
sizzling black release of ruptured oily ooze,
the smell of hair and death,
and sometimes even laughing at the yelp
when the flame came close to skin.

Nothing in that memory torments me.
A tick is a nasty creature.
Habits haunt me which they never let me witness—
the calves bawling in the barn at their castration,
the ball-peen hammer cracking the grown steer's skull.
I found the copperhead already hoed in two
beside the garden lilies.

For days my brother and I
would visit the dog's pen near the barn
to see her pups. The next day they were gone.
No grownup said a word about her whining solitude.
How did we figure out the strangling or the drowning?
I never saw, yet still see in my mind
their little whiskered faces
puckered up, eyes closed and wincing
for one more breath,
and someone's hand I loved
moving to choose another.

Relic

What old words do we remember for this lamp?
Out of someone else's past: *coal oil, wick, chimney.*
Words without a spark for decades.

It's always dim back there in childhood,
my parents' early marriage when they scrimped,
turning off every light in the house
except the kitchen table lamp
they'd bought with Green Stamps.

Whatever differences between them
might have cropped up,
they had been raised with common want.
Light when they were children
came from live fire and candle,
kerosene lamps beside their elbows
on the table shadowed evenings as they studied.

My father's mother gave me this lamp
when I married, the first she was given
to set up her own housekeeping.
Flowers etched into the base are buffed
with years of smoke and greasy soot.
The chimney shattered years ago.
The wick has petrified past lighting,
kerosene in the font gone to amber.

Hankering

In a midlife dream I was trying to kill a blacksnake,
hacking at it with a hoe along the fencerow.
As wrong a thing as I would never really do.
It slithered its sleek retreat like grace
winding onyx through the undergrowth,
thick as my wrist, nearly long as I am tall, and beautiful,
more beautiful than anything it might have harmed.
I woke up wanting to touch its silk-warm ebony
and follow the soft muscle of its meaning,
away, away, wherever.

My people raised me up with something kin to love
for what I could not understand—
a polecat's justice, hornets' revenge,
a terrapin hidden in its petite pavilion.
Everything tempted me to pry and meddle,
even the heavyweight bull that cowed
me from the corner pasture.
I would stand at the fence and bellow it a serenade.

Provocations might happen any given time—
the smell of spearmint or honeysuckle
just as likely to stop me in my tracks
as the jolt of briar to my bare feet.
I couldn't keep my hands to myself,
pestering butterflies and toads,
sneaking up on skittering birds I wanted to catch.
I handled thorns and mud on equal terms, wondering
what worm I'd budged, wondering where
each seeded milkweed dander might land,
each bit of cosmos altered from my tampering,
my footprints fugitive in the grassy dew.

Apostasy

Noah built his ark in my great-grandfather's hay barn.
And among the filthy pigs penned up outside,
the prodigal son sweated out his shameful hermitage.
There was no concordance or chronology,
no orderly testament to shepherd my mind's eye.
I traced every parable and Bible story
wandering my family's wilderness.

I imagined Baby Moses delivered from the Nile
of the South Holston River's marshy margin,
near the green shade where hidden Eden still blooms.
There is the hilltop where every miracle happened:
fishes and loaves, water into wine, ascension and burning bush,
Lazarus blinking like a lizard in the born-again sun.
There's another hill that stands in place of Ararat,
the hill where Judas hanged himself,
the hill where Abraham nearly butchered Isaac,
the hill beyond where the blood-red moon of Revelation
rose above sacred ground.

To abandon home and break my covenant
would excise every lesson's landmark,
uproot the hilltop fence where Lot's wife turned
and turned to salt.
To leave would clog the cow-pasture well
where the Samaritan woman met her Savior.
I'd make my purgatory of betrayal,
reshape the landscape where I worshipped,
erase the beatitudes my grandmother taught me.
I would relinquish my birthright, to imagine Esau
at the kitchen table eating his fill of pinto beans.
I would have to destroy the TVA dam, unleash the lake
where Jesus walked on water above drowned farmhouses.
I would have to heed Satan's offers to disown my own
and snake my tangled exodus from home.

Beyond the deed-line I was warned never to cross,
I would have to shun the sight of the steep mountain blue
where even Jesus faced temptation
and barely sidestepped the Devil's argument.

As a child I couldn't imagine wandering
forty days to see nothing but brown rocks, red rocks,
the seduction of sand for desiccated miles.
But now I have put away nearly every childish thing.
I have been to the desert to see its sky proffering eternal blue,
the delicate persuasions far from my nativity.
Now I have stood beside the ocean so wide
Christ is barely a speck, uncertain among those waves.
I have wept
to witness glaciers and tundra,
the summer prairie with uncomplicated promise.
Now I have trembled to see mountain volcanoes so vast
they would swallow up the Golgotha of my childhood.

Old House

First corpse we ever knew.

We worshiped that ancestral place
more than our ancestors themselves.

A carcass, mid-pasture without a path,
without a door, without a glass pane anywhere,
picked clean of all its wealthiest parts,
the chimney long caved into the fireplace,
the largest stones heaved out to make a raw stoop.

Inside those timber rooms,
from trees the size we never saw the likes of,
dim air lit dingy by chinked lapses.
Stair steps hung their crooked jawline,
a scaffold we clambered up
to stand and listen in the loft our parents
in their childhoods called a bedroom.

What made us stop our laugh and jabber
inside that wraith, as if we'd stepped into a funeral?
No eulogy, except the love
we couldn't dare speak,
love despite the dust and sagging,
for that stubborn palimpsest,
the same dank earth tugging at its foundation
that tugs at all of us,
bare bones set in darkness
to teach us our own history,
left standing to rot in all that tangled green,
among the daisies and Queen Anne's lace,
the vetch and high red clover.

Homesick

One time, soon after I was married, I saw a gravestone
for a man named Hill Hunter.
I can show you proof. I took a photograph
and hung it on my wall—a monument
to a monument which designates the place
on the highest hill in a rolling cemetery where
a man was put to rest whose parents named him
after places they loved, I suppose.
But for me the name is my life-large metaphor,
a designation for my own people's geographical urge.

I've been hell-bent to that hill hunting,
even in places the glacier scraped away every vestige
of a rise, not a ripple in sight higher than a field furrow—
in Ohio Amish country and the pancaked Midwest.
In Eastern Colorado, where you first spy the Rockies,
your first sight, you'll think
you're looking at the bottoms of clouds, then one more
minute-mile of disbelief, you realize you're looking
at the Plains lit up beneath horn-prick precision,
facing the relief of mountains after all.

But I could hunt my whole damned life
and never match the hills I knew and loved
when I was young, before cell phone towers
cyclopsed the horizon, and houses fattened
and proliferated and squatted to blight the richest view,
and smog yellowed the ridge lines to a smudge,
and fire and logging reshaped the knobs,
and coal-greed decapitated mountains by the hundreds.

Travel everywhere you want. I've been—
Sierras, Cascades, Alps, Pyrenees, the Ozarks;
all will teach a sort of grief,
like a widow marrying again another man
but waking every day to find herself still
a widow to the first husband, after all.

Matriarch

Our great-grandmother had died in that house.

Maybe in the same bed where we cousins spent the night,
mattress warped soft as ancestral flesh.
Across the room, our old-maid great-aunts snored
and whispered in their sleep.

It had begun to trouble us already
that virgin is only pretty for so long.

They let us stay up late to watch
Cinderella sing in her own little corner.
In just a few years, we would see
the whole affair in color.
But that young, we didn't know any better
than their muted black and white.

When someone thought we were old enough,
we learned: Their mother warned them
never to marry,
and all three sisters minded
what she said, sleeping and dying alone
in the beds where they were born.

But their dying happened long, long after
she was gone and they had grown surprisingly old.

We were grown women ourselves
by then, at their gravesites with our husbands,
safe enough from such stories.

Cross Stitch

I broke a thread across their names, no children
of my own. Maybe they looked ahead and saw that loop
that led only back to myself—a knotted dead-end.
Why teach a space-age girl to use a thimble, thread a bobbin?
They knew I'd never need a quilt frame or embroidery hoop.
Their self-fulfilled prophecy, I can barely mend
a rip or sew a button on. I make a crooked hemline.
Here I am, the clumsy dropped stitch, left-handed dupe,
unteachable. I was too contrary to spend
my lifetime handing down their seamless lifeline,
               a warp in the pattern of kin.

Field

Didn't their courage—facing
a plowed-open field—spiral me here, this
moment, to face a blank screen?
Not even a blank page,
which they might have understood,
but a white vacuum newer than a zygote,
a cotyledon, nascent
as the notion they dared to ask each season,
which alone I raise up into words:
How can there be divinity from nothing?

True believers always gather in furrows,
planting hatchling seeds, as if
a precise burial precedes
incarnation, extravagant germination,
cultivation for bellies and bones
which are fed
and gladly never fed enough.

The way that I was taught, I seek and sow
to solve the only sustenance
that can sustain me:
I work and dare this open ground again
which holds me on the planet.

Patriarch

I went to hide inside my great-grandfather's closet
and wondered there that in his life
there must have been
a long time before everybody called him Papa.

Absolutes were 2 times 2 on paper,
the infinite zones of blue, the smell of old leather
and wax, the begats and the begatted.
He was vast.

So much to be kept:
his fields kept full of green,
his cows kept inside fences,
his barns kept like cathedrals,
his yard kept inside its river-rock walls.

In his closet, time kept the night sky.
I counted ten and forgot that anyone would look for me.
Ties and two pairs of shoes, one dark suit and pants
and shirts arranged a diminishing curtain
into the dark which had no end.

He was out walking his fields and gardens,
white-headed and biblical.
Just off the kitchen, on the back porch,
that's where we all waited for him
to come in after dark, sweaty or cold from late chores.

Someone would hand him a glass
of cornbread and buttermilk
which he tinkered at with a long spoon
before he stretched his legs
and seemed to grow a little longer in his overalls,
and moved slow as the moon might move among us,
then turned up the smeared glass
and drank the last soggy crumbs,
and it was good.

The Farmers' Daughter Takes Account

If a few of them could come back
Lazarus-like and sit around a kitchen table,
I wouldn't want to know what it was like, where
they'd been. What good is news
of any sort of heaven going to do me?
I'd want to ask what they missed
while they've been gone.

It would be just before the sun comes up,
with the smell of coffee from creamy mugs they touch
lightly but seem hesitant to lift.
The light is coming. Sleep isn't gone.
Steam more real than they've been for decades,
some for a century or more.
Most I've never met. Even the ones I knew
and loved I hardly recognize, young again,
younger now than they were when I was born.

The oldest women sit, ready for milking.
Two or three of them
stand in housecoats, lean against the counter,
as if they're wondering how many men
they'll need to make gravy and biscuits for.
The men push back
their cane-bottom chairs. They're patient,
waiting for my questions, or else they fret,
as if they're at the funeral home
and dread going in to look at the body.

Their fingers are still callused, but laced and lax,
arms resting before work.
They pose as if they're set to pray, elbows
on their lanky, spread-apart legs.
They look at their feet, pondering
how strange a creature I came to be.
How I could ever
make up for the world they lost.

Mulish

That beauty of a roan horse betrayed him, raring up
like stallions we'd watched on the TV westerns.
The barn wasn't big enough for the both of them.

Back to a mule, then, common, ropey in its stance,
an ugly dun hide and yellow teeth. But sturdy,
stubborn enough to work as hard as he could.

I haven't seen a mule up close for years, not
in the shadow of the few barns still standing,
not even retired and grazing in a field.

A few towns across the country have "Mule Days,"
a testament to what we were, what we might still be
if they hadn't worked so hard to draw that load,

to rig that sluice and log the mountains
we visit and protect for leisure, where they saw
prosperity and hulking responsibility.

Sundays he dressed up fine. He sang in a quartet,
harmonizing out of books of shape-note hymns,
a tie around his neck to set the day apart,

until he died with a hundred ties and more to his name.
That's how life got lived. Work and worship.
Refuse the union. Refuse to buy a phone.

A wringer washer luxury enough for her to wash his clothes.
The indulgence of an iron for sheets and pillowcases, pajamas.
Everything in place and rows of food enough to share.

Half a lifetime ago and more since I followed along
behind that mule and plow and him in charge of all.
Half a lifetime since I helped her heft the clothes

through the wringer, change the water out to rinse.
It's a mythology, a haunted pilgrimage I make,
tending enough to their legacy to find a notion

that I might have done right by their lives, even
on ground less than sacred, leaving strange new
traces, redeeming their heavy, plodding steps.

III. Solastalgia

Sunday Afternoon: Leaving

The lunch my grandmother had cooked—
food my grandfather had gardened all summer
—sank its grit into my gut. My heart—
I could feel its small, sad working.
The two of them would stand on the carport edge
where we six had just stood.
Our foursome climbed into the car
once we'd said all the words we could say,
imagining in that flimsy hug and kiss goodbye
the eventual last goodbyes.

I could still smell my grandmother's hands
in the air, dishwater and Jergens.
His Aqua Velva.
He rolled up his shirt sleeves in the sun.

I leaned against the car window,
wondering what they'd do with themselves
without us again, watched them until
we were rounding the curve.

They stood and waved and seemed
to be brave.
They seemed to be already a chronicle.
She unhitched her apron.
He reached to fetch a wilted bud
from one of her hanging baskets.

Green

One body of lit filaments, the new wheat at the boundary
of its acreage, the very minute of the day
it grew at last as high as it would go,
leaning in pulses and urged in sunken swells, as if
it had held its breath long enough.

Then July let us all go free,
between the worry of hailstorm
and the work of picking, plucking, plowing.
The habit of weeds behind us now,
the worms daunted in the smothered shade of stalks,
the corn pointing its husks like long, cupped palms,
tobacco at rest, sweet peas and beans
at the zenith of their poles.

Green was the lazy noise the bottle flies made
on lush piles of high-summer savory manure
in pasture fields where grasshoppers lifted the sun
off their wings with every flickering sizzle.
And the river ran its forever between the high-grown banks
below the tousling jostle of sycamore and maple crowns.
The magnolia leaves gleamed their dark oily yen.
Apples like suns refused to orbit in the heat,
and the fruiting walnuts hid their promises
of dark meat high on limbs we couldn't reach.
The jarflies sermonized at dusk,
until their rasp gave way to nearly phosphorescent
singing katydids, shimmering cool chants
above the crickets' grassy, earthy *charm, charm, charm.*

Then night, when dark around the house and barns waited
in its one pure breath of sleepless sleep.
The woods without us there to witness
quavered in moss and galax, fern, ginseng, mayapple.

As if just the same we'd be perennial, and never once die,
we slept innocent as seeds in our beds.

Exodus

More people left the land than live there now.
Are you one of us, whose hands
never dig down into dirt,
who never stretches out your body
in the listing grass, just to see more sky?

Between the ground and stars
we took up such narrow room
in a narrow time,
but now in houses banked close
(as if we're afraid of leaving room enough for fences)
we've grown into exaggerated portions,
giants no one could believe walked before
with such small steps, without a trace
across the pasture to the barn.

In that gray cathedral,
in its slanted, dusty light,
we stood cousin to cousin
in bodies disappeared somewhere like husks,
weightless as those motes around us,
barely casting shadows on the scattered straw.

Territorial

Maybe we girls braced ourselves for long flight
the day we found out the land could never be ours.
The eldest boys seemed to flash like meadowlarks above us,
drifting extraordinary into the fields our fathers owned
and their fathers before. They would sing, sing, sing,
sing, sing themselves, announcing their dominion,
though we knew it already from their colors.
We pecked our browner ways in shade
and kept our voices to ourselves.
Their heads lifted under gold-tipped crowns,
free to bare their bright chests in proclamation.

Myth

They will tell stories about us.
They are already telling stories about us,
the way the Indians took scalps,
the way they say the Indians took scalps.

I have seen one,
displayed in a little old history museum, just a house
in the middle of Kansas, for one dollar admission.
But it was nothing blond.

It was the black hank from an Indian's head,
taken trophy by a homesteader.

A story is an easy mishap, misshapen
and desiccated behind glass, a worshipful,
awkward, gawked at pitiful thing.

I wanted to sniff the scratch of flesh just visible,
like ambergris, a yellow scaffold barely holding together
still the long, dusty hair somebody used to comb with love.

Any good hound will rout out blood and rot.

But who am I to raise my nose?
I can barely pick up the scent even of my own, too late
to raise the trail of the ones
who created us all from garden dust,
from roof rust in the cistern, from toolshed oil on rags
and horseshoe nails in a glass jar, from fescue rot
and corncrib must, and the attic deep with odors
of sweat and earnest piss and sometimes blood
and shit purled up in vapors along the quilt,
rising up out of the bedpan.

They used it quick and shameless,
especially on winter nights,
too cold to head to the outhouse.

Just think of the delicacy of that word, *outhouse*,
and the silence where it used to stand
at the edge of a prim row of lazy Susans.

The Robins, That Is

The generations who put me in this skin
would hardly recognize me in late April dusk
among suburban dogwoods past their bloom,
a faint delineation of the daughter they thought
to make, sitting in a meager backyard.
Just beyond my kitchen door, the noise
of passing cars obscures the reunion I came here for:
to be among the robins stirring just before they roost,
their broken, bossy syllables of plain-speak
common like my own voice talking low to them.
I try to imitate their garbled whistling in my throat
and with my lips, calling to communicate my place.
They listen for their own, but I think they tilt toward me.
I have to believe they know I'm here.

From

It's not just us here in the South
who want to know, "Where are you from?"
Everyone everywhere means,
Who are you because of the place you left behind?

If you don't want to be asked, stay home.
But fair warning:
The world will still think of you
as a stranger from a strange place
it has pared down to the simplest shorthand.

When my friend's son went to Chicago
to college, the other students swarmed him like wasps
curious for the smell of chopped wood,
cured bacon, mountain apples.
Even with his perfect scores,
they nicknamed him "Cornbread."
What else could he do but laugh?

I use him as an example in class, where
students from California and New Jersey
complain about prejudice here
in the South, about our provincialism
and narrow-minded backwardness.
They laugh at his story easily,
until I ask how their friends back home
might like being called "Taco" or "Bagel."

I have a good story to close with,
to tell about the time,
twenty years ago, I was fired from a job
in Ohio because of my accent.
Lightly as I tell it now, a sting like that never leaves.

Even in my own house, in Tennessee where
I grew up, I feel removed from
where I'm from.
There are so many answers I could give to the question.
I will tell you, just tonight, only right now,
I'm from where
I drink a nice Petite Sirah with my cornbread.

Exile

We bloomed out of the barn loft's hay mow
like one-at-a-time petals dropping.
Or some of us fell like troopers in war movies we'd seen,
parachutists sipped into the air.
Sometimes we landed sideways and fell forward
careening, just out of the way before the next one plummeted.
Clumsy, we practiced for catlike grace, the elusive sure
two-footed landing, like an anchor thrown from a great ship,
hoping to catch hold on solid ground.

Not one of us planted there. A generation gone,
making believe we could return as easily as leaping.
We limp now in late age from old wounds, fractured
consequences, torn places just now evident,
the weakened joints, the damaged
ligaments we thought would bear us up.

They Raised Big Gardens

Because not all of us learned *every man for himself,*
not even during hard times.

Because not everyone can raise up himself,
much less raise vegetables.

Because the ground was created
in the first place to feed everybody.

Because their everyday talent
was to bend with a bowed head, to kneel down.

Because there is no room for selfishness in subsistence.

Because three meals a day is not necessity
but is a necessary dignity.

Because going hungry is a better teacher
than any sermon about doing unto.

Because hunger feels like unjust punishment
just for walking, breathing, being.

Because there can always be a little left
at the bottom of every pot.

Because who gets to eat should not be a lottery.

Because we must all put in front of ourselves
on the table something to bless, by which to be blessed.

Because the table is always ready and waiting,
like a promise.

Because each mouth goes empty
most hours of the day
and needs only a bite to fill it.

Because tomorrow is too far
to go on an empty stomach.

Because the first thing we all know
is the pang of hunger.

Because among the innards,
the taste buds are sanctified,
a gift, a prodding pleasure way down
deep to stay alive.

Because it only took a few more seeds
to plant three more short rows.

Because the mule wasn't completely worn out.

Because it cost them only sweat and ache
and the effort of walking on those last few clods
in someone else's shoes.

Because the sun held the pages of June open,
promising fishes and loaves,
the light saying multitudes, beatitudes,
saying this do.

Because in the name of, for who so loved,
the meek will inherit, saying do unto the least of these,
saying unto you is given, unto you is born this day,
this very day.

At a Primitive Family Cemetery in the Great
Smoky Mountains

April woods exhume a palimpsest. I kneel
into the grape exhalation of dwarf iris,
seized like lazuli, lightning fired in blue.
Speak flowers—*trillium, bloodroot, mayapple,*
trout lily—like an echo of lost names. *Orchis,*
bird-foot violets, lady slippers. Yellow

Jack-in-the-pulpit tilts to benediction.
That dark hollow throat will borrow every elegy.
Moss-worn names on stones, faces I want whole
again refuse the tenderest resurrection,
          even on my knees in the soil.

All the Risen Mornings

Then every day was earth day,
even underneath the haunted pines,
places barely healed over on their own.
The river road still cured with wagon ruts,
darker, yawning portals to the world behind.
Everything wild and other
as willful as a newborn god demanding care—
groundhogs parsing holes,
the rabbits whiskering through garden rows,
brazen deer, thieving foxes and raccoons.
Someone had to skirt the boundary, draw first blood.

The earth would show its fist, its bloodshot eye,
craven gut, heartless heart, the selfish expectation
shrieking out in vine and rock and hail that threatened
to eat the fields alive if no one paid attention every moment.
Rats in the corn crib, and in the haymow rot and mold
tracing fast as blacksnakes along the stone foundations.

Build one fence and the ground tore down another,
native leverage taunting like the strongest hens
that plucked the weakling featherless.
The trees that swarmed hollow with bees one day
would crash the next into the roof.

The threat of moth and rust corrupted Sunday into worry
as they left the work to only six days, sacrificed
their efforts once a week, while all the while
they knew something crept,
wore through, broke down, ate up, went lost,
decrepitude devout as the mountain's high horizon.
Rain would come or not, and flood and drought and heat and fire.
A sickness might purge a whole herd—or a family.
Death was only natural, too.
Love and hunger traded jabs when they called

cows to the barn, watched the pigs
root-hog in scraps they knew they'd eat some day
in a different incarnation, feasting for the honor,
relishing the flesh of all the risen mornings
they survived and met with equal
fierce determination, like common crows
preying at the tough skin of survival.

Geometry

from the Greek for "earth measurement"

Some of us grew up in attic bedrooms
where winter mornings woke to feathered ice
along the inside of the panes.
Infinitesimal calculus of hazy crystals,
a translucent diagram of poverty.

But we had no idea we were poor,
only cold and breathing back to life
against the glass to melt the frost and rub it clear,
to see the pinking sky inside the shape our hands erased,
amorphous in its dripping null, its melting proof
that we could make our mark.

The older view, obtuse beyond us,
lived in squares and cubes and angles.
They made us sit up straight. We learned to measure
less by slant of light or hunger rumbling
and more by little clicking hands that measured out each day.

They taught us circles, spheres, and graphs.
But the parabola of our jumprope rose
and fell untouched by math.
We tested the zenith of gravity,
never thought the line from point A
to point B might mean rows of corn and beans
our parents paced off every spring at planting time,
the grid they worked to spare us from.

Who cared if Tennessee was shaped more parallelogram
than quadrilateral? We wondered only how
we'd ever cross its edges.

Our compass pointed one direction: *Gone, and never coming back.*

For the Unwritten Hillbilly Poem

Raised on the King James Version,
how could they not love every storied word
of sacrifice and blood and bloom?
But they didn't have time,
not even for the hubris it would have taken
to put beauty and anguish to rest
in their own words on the page.
The men worked alongside the beasts in the field,
busting up stumps, hugging the boulders
of their destiny, no ownership except tomorrow.
The women, like Mary and Martha conjoined,
answered the needs of every crying, mewling thing,
every budding seed and the arrogant
demands of bubbling-up yeast dough.

Servants to duty, keepers of flame and smoke,
they built up to the ridge lines and then
over yonder, progeny rising up and West and gone,
toting the smolder hearth-ash in metal buckets.
They stoked fires across two centuries
leaving barely a signature,
no moment for anything except firing pits of charcoal,
brittle black of exodus and trade
that set this pig-iron country going;
no moment between designing the delicate scaffold
of kindling under the still
and setting fields of tobacco, cured
toward the promise of a well-earned smoke;
no moment between daylight's flicker of tinder
and the whole day's dark down in the mine;
no moment between cookstove dawn and two-quilt night,
no moment between boiling the kettle for laundry
and stitching by kerosene lamp;
no moment except loading coal onto train cars
rolling in every direction like spokes on the wheel of genesis;
no moment to say rightfully what their lives were,
those rising-up, lost sparks that started America.

Kin

Is it overkill to say I love
the fragrance of these leaves
and last tomatoes on their stems?
The plants will soon be dead from frost.

I have loved. I will have loved.
I will remember having loved.

Without a child to my name,
the strongest helix I still share
is borne around by my ailing, aging parents
and my brother, half-a-century old
with gray hairs in his beard.
Who's kin is anyone, though, who swears they've
smelled the static cold of lightning long before
a July storm, maple leaves offering
their silver undersides, petrichor's clean mercy
washed across the fields before the rain.

We moved from farms and lived
in sudden neighborhoods of brick-box
ranchers, with sheetrock and a few studs between us.
We kept cold rooms for penury's sake.
Can Christmas cedar yet console our having gone?
Or wood smoke frazzled in warm fabric?
Or the bitter smell of old hay pennies
in the kitchen junk drawer?
Or meat's comfort frying in cast iron,
or the pages of an old book lifting up their must?

Listen here.
We loved. We were loved.
We remember having been loved.

The warmth we make with one sweet
breath might be enough—depending
on the syllable in that steam—to save us.

IV. Gentrification

Assimilation

Around here sometime not long ago,
we traded in *lightning bug* for the average *firefly*.
In the etymology of mountain entomology,
we've lost a few syllables here and there.
Why use three when two will do just fine?
That doesn't explain *cicada*, which we picked up
last time seventeen-year locusts came buzz-sawing around.
When we were kids, we all called them jarflies,
a poetic name enough for efficient double duty:
to name their havoc we swore
could shake black walnuts off the trees
and describe as well as their amber shells,
replicating their poses like fragile, empty glass.

Some people don't like that bug's primeval rasp
any more than they abide a primitive tongue.
In college for a degree in communications,
they enrolled me in a voice and diction course
taught by Appalachian people
who had learned not to sound Appalachian.
I couldn't pronounce "i" to suit any ear
suited toward standard pronunciation,
and so I didn't earn the A,
held back by that letter of the alphabet
which stands for me, my consciousness, my ego and my id,
the one who must stand before God alone,
capitalized in English, a totem to explain the self.

The voice I hear recorded every now and then
I don't recognize as mine,
my dialect evolving toward the six o'clock news,
avoiding the slack, condescending mimicry
I might elicit, the dreaded open-mouthed gape
or worse, that coast-to-coast question, "Are you from Texas,"
and the worst-ever, "Where the *hell* are you *from*?"

Like a chameleon, which has four syllables,
I survive by being a difficult color to read,
code-shifting as fast as a NASCAR driver changes lanes.
But in my own, preferred slow element,
I think like a hellbender, that southern mountain lizard.
My accent when I talk to my mother, my father,
my family, finds me under a cool homey rock,
nowhere near the ire that drives us to be alike.
There I can hide from the bright, shiny lights,
spiraling along the highways like sidewinding vipers,
the ones that threaten my demise.

The Other Side of the Tracks, 2016

What gentrifies most here is sky.

Dusk & musk of lilac & honeysuckle vie
for the attention of rundown houses, vine-smothered
& proliferating tiny gray-black flowers of mildew.
Or maybe what's sweet is someone's dryer running,
clean laundry despite all odds of dilapidation.
The dog leashed to a tree barks for the generic
hell of it, ignores the rabbit skimming across
the lane of broken pavement toward the creek bank.
The rooster might crow any time, day or night.

The old Black man on his tilted porch listens to AM radio—
Tony Orlando and Dawn, Jim Croce. He navigates
three squatty dogs around his lawn chair
& waves & says they never bite.
Somebody had money enough to cut down
that mangy tree across the road from his place
before its lichen-leprous body crushed the garage.
And money enough for a new steel pole in the driveway
to hoist its uncivil obsolete bluster:
Fly, Rebel flag, fly. You are confederate of nothing.
Symbol long rotted beyond resurrection.
Rabid bad blood fluttering an insurrection
of dead people's dirty laundry.

This is America duped in the sagging middle. Now,
between the highway & empty field,
beneath the regiment of transmission towers trudging.
Here no air conditioners. Screen doors open
to the muggy evening, blocked by box fans & throw rugs.

A sign lies: *Trespassers Will Be Shot.*
Three Hispanic boys play basketball in the street
with the redhaired girl whose brother is crying in his stroller.

After work the neighbors smoke &
chat across the ticking hood of a pickup & wave.
The yards glow with satellite dishes,
plastic swimming pools, and trampolines.
Bicycles make small unimpeachable promises,
where kids have left them to catch dew
& star-shine & rust.

Smell the pork chops & see the blue TV light
through windows & envy right along with them
how every place else looks from here.

Commencement

Help us not to consider our enemies flourishing
like the flowers of the field, as many as the grasses.
Help us not to imagine terror right here
as the speaker's honeyed voice lifts during the middle
of Psalm 103. As he prays, please keep us
from the distraction of the ugly inkling
that we might be deafened in the second millisecond
of the fiery blast that could shatter the gymnasium,
mangle its rage through all the bodies
gathered here in the name of our children.
Lord, help us to worship not you, but this moment
and the one before, this moment
and the one after; fill us with gratitude everlasting
for the silent peace around each word,
for the breaths we take together in congregation.
Help us take for granted the irritation
of crying babies and rude coughing and flash photography.
Fill us up with nothing but the earthy scent of our sweat,
rising up clean under graduation robes and Sunday dresses,
the suit coats of fathers and uncles and grandfathers.
Pour across us the sour smell of a thousand skidding sneakers
and the sweet odor of floor wax.
Protect us in our boredom as each name is called,
our mild applause and congratulations.
For truly this is a hollow place,
a house meant for shouting hoots and referee whistles
where worship can hardly take hold.
Lord, we are a little people, easily overlooked.
Please help others to overlook us.
Keep us safe from the monstrous in the middle of America.
Far from money and skyscrapers, please sanctify
our mediocrity, our foolish faith that no one
has any reason to harm us.
We bow our heads for the benediction
but can hardly close our eyes

against the beautiful flesh of the maple floor,
emblazoned with our home-team insignia, our colors.
Above us, the scoreboard says nothing, its clock
set at zero hour, and the basketball nets hang empty,
signs as hopeful as any you have ever given.

Linoleum Culture

There, hanging vertically
on the wall at the contemporary museum
up North, the very same pattern
my father laid in our kitchen when I was twelve.
Brown, yellow, brick-red squares and rectangles
elevated from floor to found object, a conceptual
expression about mass-production and class,
a comment on socio-economic structure
and the status of throw-away tacky.
I got it, easy, its patronizing riddle
of torn edges, a de-
construction nailed up raw,
ravaged in its salvation
from some Yankee landfill.
Nothing of its former waxed sheen,
none of the new pride we felt
watching my father unroll the geometric puzzle
he worked at for hours,
using every ounce of his educational sweat,
the algebra and calculus he taught each day
to East Tennessee's teenage brain trust, its future exports.
His brilliance measured and
cut and trimmed into practical form,
he managed the glossy upgrade we'd saved for
in one seamless unfurling,
the exact, precise dimensions of the room,
not one centimeter to spare
around the rhombus of kitchen cabinet,
parameters perfect from nook to doorway.
His pencil marks, the numerals in his hand-
writing, all hidden under the glued backing,
the mystery of his finesse and strategy
a buried marvel only our family knew,
smiling in parallel equation,
stepping carefully on his masterpiece.

In the museum, I could see clear, sure,
the artist's judgment, his assumption a pathetic reclamation.
He never could have imagined me, though,
his ideal audience, looking up,
smart enough to understand his meaning
and his accusation
from every angle.

Babel

Farsi or Arabic, Urdu, Hindustani—
I didn't know the language of staticky song
that filled our taxi until it was a wheezing lung,
like an extension of the Somali driver's body
the very pulse of his wishing as he drove
through a Minneapolis whiteout winter storm.
He had learned the distances
and meaning of a foreign climate.

If he were here with me now,
driving East Tennessee back roads,
I couldn't explain my own music,
this maudlin old hillbilly song on the car radio.
I sing along and strangle on my own self-pity,
"What are they doing in Heaven today?"
A chorus in harmony asks that lonesomest question,
a refrain that hopes without hope of an answer.

Here, I have stayed put, a good Southern daughter
suffering the slow homesickness of the loyal.
Everybody died anyway. Family scattered.
Farms sprang up their armies of brick and vinyl
like cul-de-sac graveyards. Trees we loved fell,
forests logged, skies clotted, rivers mauled.

In the song, that childhood remedy of heaven still lingers:
Maybe, maybe the whole past is just over yonder,
aunts, uncles, grandparents having dinner on the ground,
in shade and blue mountain pure air.
Would we recognize them there, waiting for us?

Lives suspend for us all on the only plane we know,
like minutes along icy Minneapolis streets,
mute beyond chants in a pleading tenor call,
sorrowful echoes ringing from the minaret.

So far from the dead he loved
the driver might have believed
that he was the one who had died,
wandering in frozen white, and that they, calling for him,
waited in a place he no longer understood.

Dead voices, maybe, they sang in an urgency
he must have wanted to join,
to follow and grieve with his own tempted tongue,
though his task was to carry this stranger
safely through in silence,
as if our mouths were sewn to.

Anasazi, the Ancient Ones

Sunset at Chaco ruins,
I eat the leftover half of my airport sandwich
but imagine native squash and corn
and beans, the same crops my own ancestors ate.

The wind-sifted grit of sand in my bread
is a way to enter here after the miracles
of taking off and landing and driving.
Seeing hardly does it.
It's a falling-down place, the round
roofless kivas and brown fine-chinked walls.
Vigas with their wood beams long rotted
make for empty-hole bird nests.
I listen and think, if that fly-over, droning plane
would stop, I might hear
the way the pueblo used to sound,
the wind and bird song, the dust.

But quiet isn't right.
A thousand people would have made noise,
a city of voices, where mothers call dinner ready,
listen for running feet, the last stick and ball
whacked on the plaza.
Listen for the clap of stone on stone,
the sizzle of wood going up in smoke like a chant.

Stillness abides the end of everything,
here in the desert the same
as in the ruins of my green mountain home,
where trees eat the sunken garden plot
and deer stand at the edge of dusk
woods without hesitation.
The house doesn't blink
under its rusted swayback roof.
There's no ax ring, no kettle sputtering on a wood stove,

no cow bawl, no milk against the metal of a pail,
no footfall creak on the stairs,
no one singing an old song at the close of day.
Who still remembers the words?
Maybe just a tune they hummed on the way
back home, like laughing out loud at the first star,
a human interruption.

The Ground Beneath Our Feet

If I stand close enough to the giant fan
sunken into the ground
beyond the woods behind my house,
can I smell the dinner buckets of the zinc miners?
Big blades rumble an outside-in
thrum like migraine, sonic shine whining
behind my optic nerves.

Can the men down there, a thousand feet,
smell the creek, the rain, October leaves turning?
All day, damselflies skitter, and toads lob themselves.
Ironweed purples the silted gleam along the bank.

Those men are not oblivious below the heaven of earth.
They drive big machines and plow drills into rock.
They change the planet inside-out, hollow
out whole caverns bigger than this town.
Channels chamber like ant hills beneath county roads
far out under cornfields gone dry now, ready for fodder.
At night the farmers dream, and their wives.
And still the mines never halt, not even for a second.

Years ago, the baseball field at the school caved in,
way in the middle of the night
when the roof of a mine shaft collapsed.
And some citizens felt they'd been spared,
and some felt they were warned,
and some imagined the worst
that could have happened but didn't,
but still might.

Look Away, Look Away

There's no stand I'm willing to take,
no living or dying I'd do in the name of Dixie,
but that war is still alive even in the new millennium,
in email jokes about dumb Yankees,
rancorous flare-ups over the Confederate flag,
in redneck comedy tours,
and even in my own sorry bile
when shiftless boys the age of soldiers
drive past and blast that truck-horn tune.

My brother tells me,
when his friend's string band
struck up that defiant cheer of home
on stage at the Knoxville World's Fair Park,
the organizer forced them to stop mid-pick.
How does it happen away down South
that we're afraid to offend even ourselves?

It's hard to keep up
with what to be ashamed of,
who's the enemy now.
The old people in our family taught me
to hate "Battle Hymn of the Republic,"
so when I was a kid I refused to sing it.
In my grandparents' living room
I read fairy tales and worked puzzles
under Robert E. Lee's watchful portrait.
They let me hold in my palm
the Minie ball my great-great grandfather coughed up
after he walked hundreds of miles home
from a Union prison camp.

On my first visit to the Lincoln Memorial
at age thirty, the marble stare accused my heritage,
that lionized story of my grandfather,

a scientist, who in his age, for all his intellect,
would not walk up those steps.

It's the autumn we elect a Black man.
At the music festival in Bristol, my hometown,
my brother plays his guitar for free
under a tent like the ones they use at camp revivals,
the ones for graveside services and re-enactments.
He's in time
with a troupe of men and women
standing around a sitting horde of men and women—
thirty or more—wielding banjos
and fiddles, brandishing dulcimers and mandolins,
the standing bass fiddles on guard at the outskirts.

In the streaming street, out in the sun,
hard-won places are taken up in the crowd
by dark-skinned faces—Latino families,
a group of women dressed in saris.
There's the smell of kabobs
bearded men sell across the street
and a new Chinese restaurant
in the next block, with a line out the door.

Sometimes one of the musicians gives a whoop
over the ringing strings,
a Rebel yell newcomers might not recognize.
But it's a brutal kin to other anthems
kept alive in other civil places,
where the soil of battlefields
still comes up blood-soaked—   .
Croatia, Kashmir, Rwanda,
Tiananmen Square and Darfur,
Kandahar and Fallujah,
Wounded Knee.

The players shout and don't stop playing,
though their hands must ache,

their fingers blister and rupture.
Without singing, they play the old tune
they know by heart
over and over and over, until it seems harmless,
until it sounds almost perfectly joyful.

Sushi for Hillbillies

It's posh in East Tennessee tonight.

Thursday maki rolls are half-price
and all-American—tempura deep-fried
with cream cheese, smoked trout, and sauce that's nothing
if not mayonnaise's kissing cousin.

In line for the ladies room, these two are Pentecostal,
one with untrimmed lank and holy hair,
the other with a braid hanging nearly to the hem
of her acid-washed blue jean skirt.
She's preaching over again what she preached
to some poor man who's lost and bound for certain.
"I told him, if you sin, you're going to hell.
There's nothing to it besides that."

It's a thin vein of roe that calls us home,
reminds us of the smallmouth bass we split open
long ago on some rickety back porch table,
in view of the cow field and the river
rising up into fog against the mountains.

Now we dine on precious flesh we must practice
to pronounce: *maguro, ikura, unagi, nori,*
daikon some local boy juliennes
to earn eight bucks an hour.

This is the extravagance that tempted me
when I used to make-believe grown-up,
wishing my parents owned martini glasses,
praying someday I'd cross over
to that other, blissful side, sophisticated and redeemed.
Now we've all arrived, our coveting accomplished.
We're proud our Southern portions are on equal terms

with tender bites they pinch in chopsticks
from Santa Barbara to Boston.

But we're like koi, those giant goldfish transformed,
our copper scales grown crimson, larger
and outgrowing, bound forever round and round,
a swelling fatuous luxury
of being bigger than the day before,
in those same backwaters where
we were bred, still circling.

The Hard Stuff

Wild berry-infused, cherry-tinctured, peach-laced,
no matter what flowery flavors of new-millennial distillation,
moonshine will forever be part spectral myth,
part hobgoblin stereotype.

Now black-market bootleg elixir is all costumed up
and legal, bonafide trickster after all those revenuers died,
after all the murderous chase and jail time
and Popcorn's tragic suicide—that elvish scofflaw.

Corn liquor or sour mash or white lightning,
renegade black-sheep brother of bourbon,
redheaded stepchild of vodka,
there's no exorcism for home remedy.
That phantom animates us, our fine reputation,
even against our will.

Ghostly colorless Mason jars
wait suspended in some dark hidey-hole cupboard,
tucked behind the spider-webbed
basement-corner work bench,
lurking in the serpent's lair of the home file cabinet,
brew as clear and harmless as water,
inert as a lie, until it hits the tongue
and the throat catches fire,
and full possession lights the mind like a haint.

Civil Ceremony

My cousin's daughter believes at first that it's a joke
her mother is telling over ham and Jell-O salad
after yet another family funeral.
Then her face goes a little ashen, mouth hinged open.
It's true. Our wedding receptions took place here,
in the church's musty block-wall basement.
Folding tables laid with white paper cloths
and silver bowls of butter mints and mixed nuts,
lime-sherbet punch in borrowed glass cups,
a sheet cake cut in dainty squares
to make enough to go around.

We stop our storytelling before she faints,
a girl already sleepwalking exclusive venues
in her designer beaded gown, idling over champagne toasts.
Raised on pageantry, her imagination disavows
receiving lines on gray linoleum.
She will dance on dazzling marble floors.

She'd never believe that no girl *ever*
didn't wear white. As upright frugal
as we were chaste, flanked by bridesmaids
in homemade pastel, garden gladiolas in the urns.
The biggest splurge our fathers' cramped new Florsheims.

But then we can't help auditing wedding stories
this day we bury our next-to-last great-aunt:
She married at sixteen
in a civil ceremony, widowed before she turned fifty.
Her single wedding photo shows her
giddy in pragmatic tweed, as if to match his suit coat,
a fedora tilted jaunty on her head.
Is it his hat? They are starting out their life
sharing a boisterous joke.

Her last years she moved back home
to live with her eldest sister.
She'd been called an "old maid" until
she married for true love the first and only time
at sixty-two, widowed only eight years later, bereft.
The afternoon her old groom came to pick her up
to head to the courthouse,
her gray-haired sisters ran out to his Chrysler
and teased like school girls:
"Mama's decided she's not going to let her go!"

Think what they must have talked about
each morning, two widowed sisters meeting
in the kitchen like an old couple.
They plugged in the percolator and set out their mugs,
looked out on the weather of the day, deciding together
whether to fix oatmeal or toast,
and the eggs scrambled, or sunny-side up maybe,
or maybe even—for that rare extravagance—coddled.

Birthright

My friend Doug takes photographs of retired farmers
having their morning coffee now at McDonald's—
either the one in town or out on the interstate.
They used to meet up for breakfast
at a place called TW's when they were young farmers,
before their barns caved in
and they sold their land to be subdivided.
Or they'd take their wives out once in a while for little square
hamburgers by the bagful at a joint
called Pops, before Sonic and Krystal, before Taco Bell
and Hardee's and KFC, and 24/7 corporations
lined the highway through town, with Walmart
and the banks with their plantation architecture and ATMs.
Their sons and daughters and grandkids
work the grills & fryers & drive-through windows.

The fields that used to be full of bees and buttercups
in May are open red gashes with clods, waiting
for the next business or subdivision
or windowless factory—which we'll be glad for.
Like the power plant, it'll top the highest hills,
the best places in this little town
for a panoramic view of the mountains.

Hillbilly Ghazal

The *"n" word* is a noose, even unsaid, tongue quick to silence,
choked and blue. Hate can make for a tricky silence.

Be blunt inside your head, and still you'll dangle, dead weight
at the end of your own rope, hanging thick in silence.

Hide the slanderous names, but history holds a mud pit, slung
with *dago, towelhead, heeb, fag, cracker,* ugly slick with silence.

Irish, Catholic, white-trash poor with heavy brogues,
the million branded scatterlings withstood *Mick* in silence.

El rio es un camino. Thousands swim against their
native tongue. They answer *wetback* and *spic* with silence.

Wars linger in the lies of movies. The back end of history
interns the sacrifice of *Jap* and *chink* and *gook* in silence.

Accept and acquiesce. Ignore the dirty names gone threadbare
up the ranks, until—unanimous—we're politic with silence.

You think the slur you think is just a thought. The ones you vilify
will never be so wise to guess: Your stones and sticks are silence.

Words will murder from the inside out. I hear you think it.
You might as well say it. Call me *hick.* Break your silence.

Specter

Associate those days with hives of bees,
blacksnakes along the hewn foundations of barns.

It is a conjugation of memory.

We ran through the mowed yard
and flung the dark aside with sparklers,
singeing phosphorescent lines into the black,
a fleeting alphabet of who we were.

They told us others answered those names before us,
the gruesome old and put-away dead.
No one would ever catch us just by calling.
The grass went cool to easy dew
beneath our pommeling feet.

Sometimes they even said—as if in verse—whose feet,
whose toes, whose eyes, whose hair.
They disagreed.
"No, he looks just like himself,"
someone would finally declare, as if it were a joke,
a lie, a lesson yet to come.

We never owned a toy big as that nighttime,
ignited in frivolity of flesh and fire,
the smell of gunpowder on our fingertips.

Our lights sizzled, white-blinding us
to where they waited,
saying things we couldn't fathom
while we burned the last minutes to pieces,
until finally we had no excuse except to come inside,
but not until every last
shriveled dust of wire was spent.

Splinter

Their scars amazed us, silver sinewy gouges
deep in forearm, calf, or thigh,
and sickly pink cankers left like bubbled burns.
How could they have stood the pain? And worse,
the lifetime ugliness they wore as effortless as perfect skin.
More garish, still, each healed-over pock had its own story—
blood and gash without a doctor for miles.
No stitches. The old ones poured on turpentine
or kerosene, which wounded
worse than wounds themselves.

They lived to tell how good we had it,
mercurochrome and stingless sprays
and bandages beneath fluorescent lights.
Our mothers kissed our elbows,
blew cool breath across scraped knees.
They wiped away our useless crying.

Tonight a splinter plunged into my knuckle,
a half-inch deep without surprise, a tiny recognition.
I picked it till it bled. I pulled and prodded.
Forty years ago I would have wailed.
Only pain has taught me callousness like this,
only long days of fever. Suffering.
The weeks of blood I've lived.
And worse than funerals, the death bed visits.

A scar is a worthless reminder of pain.

Instead I want to know again my innocent mind,
my tenderness, my skin before it ever scabbed.
I want to go back there and ride in the backseat
with the windows rolled down.
I want that day back I was ten,
when we topped the hill and saw the road

to my grandmother's house ruined
with a yellow line painted toward the future.
I want to weep and weep like that again
for the damaged world to come.

I Stand Here Frying Okra

Not in my grandmother's skillet,
but sizzling in my new-millennial non-stick.
And not on her rewired, cantankerous electric eye,
but on my stainless dual-fuel Jenn-Air,
in corn oil tempered with fine imported olive oil.
I didn't traipse like she did downhill to a garden
toting a dented bucket and a half-rusty knife,
or reach high on stalks for living furry pods.
This okra cost three dollars a pound, organic,
laid cleanly cool like newborn gods in baskets
within my fingers' reach.

Standing at my kitchen counter under daylight-balanced light,
I slice lengths two-by-two with my Japanese ceramic knife
against my bamboo cutting board, swipe the angular circles
into a clean-white porcelain dish.
Not at all the way she did, sitting
in the languorous dim afternoon at her kitchen table,
elbows to the sides of her old stainless bowl,
okra *ping-pinging* as she cut in mid-air
with a paring knife against the callus on her thumb.

She wouldn't have known what to do
now they've stopped milling Three Rivers meal.
It's left to me to make do with Martha White,
okra tumbled through my fingers, coated pale
and set to rest while hot oil puddles up its shimmer.

When the dusted rounds hit grease, they send up
memory's own pheromone, hay-green late summer.
Years after she is gone, I follow her best secret:
settle on the lid to steam. Be patient.
But I can hardly wait
before I crank the flame to blue and with my spatula
at the ready, shake the pan as if it's popcorn.

The crisp, raw green singes tender gold, edges toward brown.
When there's no resisting—when I think for half a second
she might yet show up to catch me—
I pinch into the pan and blow
on one morsel, tossing palm to palm.
Palm to palm. Then the savor of childhood
bright and vivid as her voice.
Each bite will taste exactly like her okra did,
out of the old, nearly lost salt-comfort,
robust as a living pulse on my tongue.

Acknowledgments

Alaska Quarterly Review: "Appalachian Diaspora"
Appalachian Heritage: "Apostasy"
Appalachian Journal: "Holler"
Appalachian Places: "Geometry," "Homesick," and "Old House"
Chapter 16: "Look Away, Look Away"
Now & Then: "Territorial"
Oxford American: "Babel"
Pea River Journal: "Specter," "Splinter," and "Tick"
Poetry South: "I Stand Here Frying Okra"
Red Branch Review: "Sushi for Hillbillies"
Roanoke Review: "The Robins, That Is"
The Southern Poetry Anthology: Tennessee: "Assimilation," "For the Unwritten Hillbilly Poem"
Still: The Journal: "Ghazal of the Farmers' Daughter," "Cross Stitch," "The Farmers' Daughter Takes Account," and "Exodus"
Town Creek Poetry: "Commencement"
Tusculum Review: "Myth"

"Holler" was printed as a broadside in 2014 and appeared in the Women of Appalachia Project's anthology *Women Speak*, Vol 8 (Sheila-Na-Gig Editions, 2022).

A few poems here were previously included in the chapbook *From*: "Anasazi, the Ancient Ones," "From," "Babel," "Linoleum Culture," and "Look Away, Look Away" (Finishing Line Press, 2010).

About the Author

Susan O'Dell Underwood is a native of East Tennessee, where she has lived most of her life. She's the director of creative writing at Carson-Newman University. She has published one earlier collection, *The Book of Awe* (Iris Press, 2018), a novel, *Genesis Road* (Madville Publishing, 2022), and two chapbooks. Her poems and fiction have appeared in journals and anthologies such as *A Southern Poetry Anthology: Tennessee*, *Oxford American*, *Alaska Quarterly Review*, *Tupelo Quarterly*, and *Still: The Journal*.

www.ingramcontent.com/pod-product-compliance
Lightning Source LLC
Chambersburg PA
CBHW032206010726
47493CB00008BA/2851